Combed by Crows

poems

Dennis Camire

DEERBROOK EDITIONS

PUBLISHED BY
Deerbrook Editions
P.O. Box 542
Cumberland, ME 04021
www.deerbrookeditions.com
issuu.com/deerbrookediitons

FIRST EDITION

Page 95 constitutes an extension of this copyright page.

ISBN:978-0-9975051-6-0

Book & cover design by Jeffrey Haste.

Contents

I

Beautiful Dying Things

Ode to Teenagers' Hairdos in June

Today the teens bouqueting faces
From the gazebo's railed vase
Have hair shaped into flowers
Whose Latin roots escape
The brain's gray matter

As this girl's blue-highlighted curls
Turn her into a psychedelic tulip
And this boy's orange and black-dyed spikes
Morph him into the world's tallest marigold
Whose eyebrows dragonfly with delight.

It's as though they're playing out
Some pagan ritual they intuit
And the purple and green roots
Have nothing to do with hormones rollor-
Coastering the cardiovascular—

Or it's as though the hair
Literally has a mind of its own
And will blossom its exotic beauty
Despite how they might pass-out
On the life raft of their lover's mattress.

And today, with the yellow periscopes
Of Russian sunflowers' a month away
And spring's purple iris wrinkling
Under dry, summer skies
Even the mother with

Down's syndrome child in tow
Slows to marvel
At this Garden of Eden of Teens
Before sitting by the river's magic carpet
Where she thinks her hair, soon,

Will be a strange off-gray or blue
As she still cares for the son
Who'll never color his hair green
Though, in his fifties, likely,
Still seduce her into this world's strange beauty

The way he always blossoms
That same smile to each unexplained glory
Which, maybe, she now realizes,
Is the only flower any mother could desire
Growing over her grave

Under the iris blue sky
That, too, on our best day
Often feels like the perfect hairdo
Though held in place
And fine-tooth-combed by crows . . .

Severely Autistic Bagboy Asking Out Check-out Girl

After she says “no” to “arcade games
And ice cream cones,” she only longs for him
To feel her heart breaking, too, in seeing
How honesty isn’t proportionate to smarts

As she lies about the college boyfriend
Driving up for homecoming weekend
And sees how his rejection hurts more
Because he'll never letter in a sport

Or French kiss a cheerleader under
The bleachers. And, when he’s then
Apologizing for just wanting someone
Smarter than himself, she just wants to know

How to double-bag her own emotions
As she feels so dumb for being the one
Weeping at the end of this transaction
And needing his shoulder to lean on

Before accepting his offer to walk her
To her car where he guides her into the
Seat, she thinks, gently as a bag of groceries—
As though he knows her empathy

And kindness are so fragile from being
Shaken from temperature-controlled aisles
And he’s thinking of the widow, Mrs. Jones,
Whose ice cream sometimes doesn't survive

Her long, slow, drive home . . .

Watching the Man with No Arms Teach the Boy with No Arms How to Fish

With toes resembling fingers
Of an ambidextrous masseuse,
His left foot grips the pole
While he sits on the beard of beach

So, when the
            Bobber dimples
Under with fish,
            He sets the hook with a karate kick

While two right toes
Reel in the largemouth,
And the ten-year-old
(Who's soon to brood

Over how it must feel
To translate the Braille
Of a woman's body into the
Tongue of each fingertip)

Is impressed
Over how this man suddenly makes arms seem
Gratuitous—
Claps his little foot soles

Before stepping over
The scales of the
Shimmering abdomen
So the man's toes can

Tip-toe
Down
The bass's
Throat

To unfasten
The barbed
Hook . . .
And convincing him

Self-esteem
And upward mobility
Have nothing to do
With two good arms,

Soon we're seeing video
Of the boy steering
A two-wheeled bicycle
With his mouth.

But, it's when we realize
How an army of arms
Aren't enough to keep us
Embraced to this sudden wild sense

Of gratitude and reverence,
That we embrace, paint
Each other's back with
Fingertips of touch,

And, like the boy, hope
We can learn to reel in
Such a beautiful
Frightened being.

Watching the First-time Seeing Eye Dog Trainer Part with Her First Dog

After three years of teaching
The Labrador to guide her through
Subways, carnivals, and malls

And discern which restroom
Is male or female—just moments
From losing the only roommate

Who makes her feel safe
From another attempted rape,
It's no wonder she takes solace

In how the blind man can't see
The tears irrigating her grieving face
Or know her recurring dream

Where her lab. retrieves his instinct
To retrieve beautiful dying things
And braves twenty miles of highway

To lick her latte-flavored lips
At the 4th street bookstore and cafe.
Yes, suddenly so fetched by her affection

For a companion who saw her through
The night of her sister's suicide
And who never said "let's just be friends"

Those evenings he was the only one to call
For a walk through the moon-frosted park,
It's not hard to see why she feels

In need of guidance back to
Her two-room, walk-up studio
As, half-blinded by sorrow,

She tries exiting through the entrance
Then crossing against the light . . .
On her way, she realizes,

To weeks of freezing by the hydrant
He always sniffed twice
And seeing, as she slowly walks away

And her tender memories won't "sit
And stay" despite her repeated entreaties,
That, maybe, it's this love

Which always heels just behind us
And, in the end my friend,
Really is man's/woman's best friend.

Retinitis Pigmentosa

—for Rebecca Veeck and her parents

Watching their child go blind
The parents quit six-figure incomes
Cash in stocks and bonds,

And give their daughter the gift
Of composing a list of all she desires to see
Before her vision is just the love child

Of memory and imagination. And at eleven
The girl begins with the usual: Disney World,
Old Faithful, the Statue of Liberty.

But inspired by her parents' PhD's
The list soon includes the Gardner Museum
And a complete T-Rex skeleton

As the parents peer into her future
And consider what vista or Vermeer
Might appear in her mind's eye

When she's about to swallow the pain
Killers. Oh, their belief in the power of beauty
To preserve a human soul

As beautiful as anything you've ever seen;
Their hope that beauty might open
A pre-teen's third eye as grandiose

As Michelangelo imagining
"The Creation of Adam."
But, soon, with savings draining,

They're choosing between
Egyptian tombs or Mayan ruins
And debating the value of watching

Salmon struggle against a fall
Or bats tornado from a cave
And fly blind through the night—

Until, on the plane ride home
They're blindsided by their girl weeping
Over wanting "to go home

To spend her remaining vision
Memorizing the smiles of friends
And the mountain view from her room"

Instead of trying to see all
The beauty our world holds.
And see, now, how each parent lingers

Over the mental photo of that moment
As long as they lingered over Picasso's
"Absinthe Drinker" and "Blind man's Meal."

Like you wanting to remember
The genius it took to extract such meaning
And beauty from her like suffering.

Like you, almost fearless of the darkness
They know hides behind the closed
Lids of their own horizon

Now that their child has finally
Given them the unexpected gift
Of simply seeing this.

The Beauty of the Last Cutthroat Trout of the Season

Sets widowers and divorcees musing
'If they knew it'd be their last time
Rubbing their lover's own soft belly,
They'd have lingered longer
In the tributaries of sex, gazed deeper
Into her like sky-capturing eyes,

And blessed their union in
That same raging wetness'—
Instead of smoking or watching TV
And feeling, now, regret's
Own bottom-feeding eels nibbling
At the end of each longing thought's line

So that, foreseeing at least six moons
Until the next cut throat rainbows
Over the stream, the anglers lament
All the like ice-time until the next lover arrives
Though, filling the new reel over winter,
The green, floating line—they dream—

Might teach them how to let
Their future tender thoughts float over
The surface of their emotions'
Own chaotic run-off. And the bamboo poles
Carved and sanded to a hundredth of an inch
Might foretell of the flexibility they'll bring

If the next lover too, insists grandkids
Need be, for a time, her main priority.
Yet no old, hip-wading angler, now,
Expresses this blessed entangling
Of fish, love, and metaphysics
So that it's an art kin to fly fishing

For you to glimpse the tenderness
In their gentle plying of pliers in
Removing the hook of the black ghost—
Or for you to note the lingering
Of fingers over the slick, fat, dappled back—
Or for you to see the gift of them

Offering you to kiss the wet nose
Before their inarticulateness of "well, you know,"
Or "freezer space needed, I guess, for deer meat"
Uttered in response to you musing "Why
Would you let such a beautiful old cutthroat,
So late in your fishing life, go?"

Stephen Hawking at Zero Gravity

Aloft I'm a fetus   flotsam in the
Amniotic fluid of a third- trimester womb—
Then like a volleyball   as I waft
Above the constellations   of heads
Then watch them softly   nudge my feet
And fetal torso—just so-—
To keep me
From hitting the wall.   But when they toss
A red delicious   in tribute to me
Defying Newton, I turn into Pluto   caught
In the grav-itational pull   of a fiery Jupiter
Or become a constellation   I'll name
"Stephen Hawking Gawking."
Now, too, their tears of gratitude
Seem to crash, like meteors,
Into the   atmosphere
Of my blue-moon   jumpsuit
So, as my arms open   in embrace
For the first time in   decades
It's "me" weeping   over all the love
I never dreamed   rising so beautifully
From so many earth-bound bodies
As the "crew" achieves the zero-
Gravity of complete   empathy
And their "ahhs" and "oh my gods" rocket
Into my smile's Milky Way   swirl . . .
And, let me forever feel
Like   that orbiting satellite
Keeping tender words flowing
Between lovers in separate hemispheres
So, if I could speak, I'd recant   my slight
About me "still searching earth   for signs
Of intelligent life"   for see how, eight times,
I rose and fell like   an angel in training
Until coming to love   the slow de-scent
As much as this out-of-body-rising

For how—the earth's awaiting   gravity
And my disease—only sank me
Deeper   and deeper
Into their weightless embrace.

For Retired Astronauts Falling in Love

How they cherish feet not seeming

To touch the ground when their

New beloved is around—or, say, how

Those starry bedroom eyes looking down

Are like constellations which turned

The cramped pod into a cradle rocked,

That first night in space, by some God--

So new love, for old cosmonauts,

Is the yearned-for return to the

Breath-less-ness of space exploration

Where the soul is nothing less than a Solar system

One can only begin to know after

A lifetime of training and dedication;

And as they don date night's moon-suit

Of new blazer and buffed, leather shoes

While embracing their passion's vastness

Also pulsating with Super Novas of emotions

(Which, too, seem to need a million years

To burn to their death), the Houston

Of our yearning re-launches our wish

To be these same fearless space sailors

Not nauseous during the first date's rocky take-off

Or worried how the gravity of past heartache

May have savaged our precious bodies;

And we vow, next time, when just espying

A twinkling eye across the room

To bourbon-rocks-booster- rocket to

The distant constellation of their face

Where so many unidentified flying emotions

Are rumored to fly by night and, sometimes,

Drive star gazers mad with delight;

And as another seventy-plus rocketeer

Moonwalks down the aisle for the third time

In honor of desire's own speed-

Of-light-expansion creating another

Galaxy of gladness, we vow, finally,

To overlook all the painful re-entries

Of break-ups which left us trapped in

A shot glass's wobbling pod of whiskey—

Or isolated as the researcher left, for months,

In the space station's lab—even if we know,

At our age, we might never again suspend

So playfully over the space dust of our lust—

Or reach that distant Red Mars or Venus

Of another's wise, ancient heart—

Or, making our way through

The 90% dark matter between any two

Humans seeking love and union

Discover a more intelligent form of life.

Stephen Hawking Talking (to Lou Gehrig)

—after reading Albert Goldbarth's *Stephen Hawking Walking*

Oh Lou, to gracefully walk away
From my all-star fielding of galaxies
Praising "how lucky I feel" to have played
In a Milky Way that takes a quarter-billion years to
Complete a single revolution

Though I'm still grateful to Prime Mover
The light of these lines through
The computer's infinite cosmos of chips
And watch eyes supernova delight
As my synthesizer decrees to

A roomful of students "how the human
Body contains enough D.N.A.
To stretch to the sun and back a dozen times."
But tonight, with just a page of scribing
Turning into advanced aerobics

For my crippled fingertips,
How hard to forget I'm being swallowed whole
By my personal black hole . . . Oh,
Iron Horse who followed Ruth in the line-up
And decreed you were "the luckiest man

On the face of the earth," appear
In my "quantum field of dreams"
To reveal how a divine mind
Underlies the galaxy
Of my 3-billion lettered genome

Where only 3 defective atoms keep me
From being completely normal!
Imagine me a cosmology of the body
Placing the diseased planets of my genes
At the center of God's benevolent vista!

Yes, tonight, just one more lecture
Where my vocal chords "cello"
My hardened torso
As I sing of "all the bones' calcium
Coming from a supernova burning to its death."

Tonight, just one more moment in time
Where I praise "the North star's light
Beginning its journey to my eye
Around the time Shakespeare
Was scribing all those wonderful plays"—

The line, Lou, I used before
Proposing to my wife who,
Night gowned in moonlight, swore
My voice came down from the
Very hierarchies of Dante's Paradisio

Whose stars, moons, and planets too
Are beautifully expanding through infinity
Even though—to the human eye—
Seemingly paralyzed
And silent as the light.

The Dry Stone Waller Muses About Cosmology

For God, stars and planets are like set stones
Whose poetic constellations balancing
On nothing but the grace of gravity
Mark the line between human and divine,
And we, like creatures in dry stone walls, thrive
In the negative space between earth and moon—
Venus and Las Vegas—though, yes, true,
Like lizards, frogs, and mice—we still fear being
Crushed by the errant meteor, or wonder—
Like chipmunks trembling to waller's hammering—
If a kind being is behind this grand design
Which sometimes frost-heaves with tsunamis
So, some days, we see the meek, lowly snail
As one of God's chosen people as she
Carries her adobe home on her shoulders
And, when retreating from the white light
Of probing finger, finds her only hope in
Her molten body hardening into stone.

II

Crumbs Thrown from a Benevolent God

The Single Mother and the Meteor Shower

Under the blueberry field's Big Sky
Where they picked high bush
The summer prior to the divorce,

She dreams of composing
A mother/son memory
Which makes grand re-entry

Each time, as a rebelling teen,
The boy's tempted to blame
His every truancy and failing grade

On his divorced, working mom
Whose two job-related moves
Pulled him from three consolidated schools

Just when he'd made a best friend.
But each time a meteor welds
The night sky's steel,

The boy's gazing
At the constellations in
The hand-held video game

Instead of a Milky Way
His mom claims
"Takes a quarter-billion-years to complete

A single revolution."
And so by the time
The first owl U2's the field

And the boy rolls into the comforter's
Sweet cannoli of sleep,
The mother sees

Her grand plan dissolving
Like meteors entering
Our oxygen-

Happy
Atmosphere
And she's seeking hope

In those ancient sailors
Navigating oceans
Via Hercules and Andromeda

Though their stars, she knows,
Are speeding from one another
Thousands of miles per hour . . .

Yet, preparing to leave
The sky's sea of electric eels,
Maybe the meteoroid

Of a future memory's trajectory is set
The way the boy suddenly wakes
To spy tears streaming

From his mom's eyes
And, asked why she's crying,
The mother can think nothing

Other than to whisper:
"Honey, I just wanted you,
Finally, to see something beautiful."

Teaching Simile at a Midwestern University

I said "you need to see a feather
As a tree in the forest of pheasant."

I tried fusing the two brains with
"A watch is like a moon with a mind."

And a few went on to write:
"A purse is like money's mouth"

And "a crow flying to road kill
Is like the Grim Reaper's directional."

But most feared simile disguising
Those Magnum-Opus emotions

In those essays about being
The only lesbian in Midland, Kansas

Or desiring to fail senior history
Because they hadn't a parent

To snap the photo when the diploma
Was batoned into their palm.

My graduate student challenge:
To convince them simile isn't like

A burka placed over a wife's face
To mute the contempt that likely

Stamens from her gaze. Oh, frustrated
With their continued frustration,

I felt like the soccer coach
Making players follow-through

On all those strange yoga poses
Moments before the championship game—

Or like the Zen master stressing breathing
To the novice seeking to see the Buddha

In the next lotus he walks over.
But gratefully that mid-western university

Allowed for my own improvement
And future lessons in simile found me

Playfully vivifying things with
"The heart is like an accordion

Too few of us learn to make sing
Though the left and right brains press

So many buttons and squeeze
A sleuth of keys." And gleaning

The possibility of simile filleting
Some of those salmon-pink feelings

One imagined "desire like the scarlet runner bean
Clinging to pole and chicken wire."

Another saw "the heart as a catcher's mitt
In the fast-pitch league of adult relationships."

But it's how most come to trust
How truth can be beauty

And how beauty can be truth
As one or two always secret you

Poems or essays where a simile or two
Releases some of the pain

From their mother's suicide
Or guilt from their ninth-grade rape

That has me saying to you: "it's true;
You do learn so much from your students

For just like I was saying to
My teacher-friend Marita:

Sometimes there's just nothing to
Compare the beauty of these students to"...

For the Russian Rainbow Trout Farmer

Circling the holding cage's docks at dawn
He muses on the confined rainbows below
So kin to his pent up hopes to be a poet

Not rifling through the white waters
Of a morning's inspiring lines rife
With the spring run-off of Jungian dreams

Cresting with archetypes. And envying
Their wild leaps, at dusk, to nothing but
The pocked spinner bait of a quarter moon,

Reveals his need to break free from "net profits"
So he might, too, re-inhabit the vast
Lake Kiev of his childhood imagination.

Still, squeezing eggs from his fall brood stock,
Inspires "dotted backs like galaxies under glass"
So he feels filled with the roe of his own poems . . .

Until feeding now, each morning, inside
The holding pond of an anthology of sonnets,
Emboldens him to ignore the next break in the cage

So he can feel his own rainbow soul es-
Caping to the spring-fed mountain streams
Of the Greek muses descending. Bless, then,

This odd farming of his own heart illuming
The faux pink fillets of our work places
And schools' factory raised imaginations.

And praise the trout totem he'll soon carve
In reverence of these wild creatures
Never ceasing to press their noses to the

Steel mesh between them and the river's
Underground Railroad delivering them
From their lake incarceration. And when he then

Begins releasing a few fingerlings, each Friday,
Consider his hands lingering in the river
To savor the promise of his own return

To the currents of his words' flowing—
Where his cursive verbs, we pray, leap
With the same passion of a rainbow

To his first dragonfly in May;
And where the heart's compressed feeling
Within each stanza's taut line,

Is a lush pink fillet which will sate
Our appetite for high protein feeling;
And where everything he, too, ever desired

Or daydreamed while trapped within
A life's 9 to 5 confines, is, maybe, nothing less
Than his natural state, finally realized.

Moose Ode

French kisser of bogs,
Rainbow trout, and polliwogs—
Brothel for black flies
Mosquitoes, and fleas—train derailer,
Epicenter, and slow, soft gazer
With a beard resembling that
Of the turkey and the Yogi—
With the crown of a corrupt
Colonial king, the patience
Of Job, the sadness
Of a Post-Modernist, the legs
Of a llama, and the ears
Of a deer—you are so strange
You could be
God.

Widow Feeding Seagulls

Hovering over like a giant halo
Which shrinks to her head size
As the tossed bread-crumbs

Descend, she feels like Saint Assisi
With those sublime sparrows
Alighting his cloaked shoulders

And soon sees, too, how she's feeding
With like greed on all
The grace in those airy wings

Softly brushing her head and elbows—
Like the ex, she thinks, who swooned
In, each Saturday, for sex

No matter how stale her words
Of foreplay. And the way the gulls
Descend each Maine, winter morning

Like an legion of angels
Even when the lilac, purple sky
Daggers rain, sleet, or snow,

Any wonder she comes to believe
The birds are a handful of crumbs
Tossed from a benevolent God

To console through grief's coastal gales
And loneliness's own sandy beach
Always in erosion....

So, when dog walker or jogger
Pass her by the granite breakers,
She's exuding such gratitude

For this daily communion
That'll soothe through the noon tea
And evening's rosary taken alone

That all stop for her offering of crumbs
To toss, in kind, into sea breeze where it coaxes
The halo to merry-go-round over

And, like each brush with grace,
Trail one a short while after the final,
Stale wonder bread is swallowed whole.

Earthworm Poem

As children we'd incarcerate
These blind miniature snakes
Inside the fist's solitary confinement
Then marvel at their braille-
Reading nose always finding the escape-
Hole between pointer-finger and thumb. Later,

Our fascination with their five hearts
Inspired us to raise the squirming
Earrings of them to our ear lobes
In hopes of hearing a few notes
From the neck's orchestra of organs . . .
Until, a grade or two further—learning

Of the amazing tail regeneration
After bird scissors it below midriff—
We saw how our awe for these earthy eels
Would, too, always regenerate to squirm
Through the brain's gray matter
Despite all the packed asphalt of our learning

So that, maybe, we might trust
That continued urge to emerge
With flashlights rainy nights
To wander the gravel drive
And rescue these near-drowned beings
Into the ICU of compost pile—

Where, kneeling, now, as they burrow
Through eggs and coffee grounds,
We finally digest the miracle
Of a million of these slick,
Soil factories below each tilled acre
Replacing two inches of dirt

Each growing season;
And with soil scabbing our knees
And our own fingers worming
Into dirt, feel a like blessedness—
A birth—in our own blind returning
To our beloved earth.

The Gardeners' Widows

And so, soon after planting their last rows,
Thousands of gardeners' hearts are harvested
By the organic gardener of God
So their wives then spy their loved one's eyes
In all the squash and zucchini blossoms
Batting their bee-wing lashes. And, by June,

Some espy his beloved pole beans winding
Up the corn stalk's lithe thigh and they long—in the night—
For his snaking embrace of their old torso
Until, by July—with flowering potatoes
So aloft like the first bouquets he gave
To umbrella their love—a few, as at the wake,

Need to turn away from this open casket
Of cherry tomato cheeks and cucumber thumbs
Resting over the mounds' of his burgeoning pecs.
Now, some let the weeds overtake turnips
So large, red, and split apart, they think
As his artery-hardened heart; others prune grief

By clipping melon vines which too much remind
Of his own endless sweetness in reaching out
To snow blow the shut-in, neighbor's driveway.
Still, despite the sadness of that summer's salads,
A few delay that final 'goodbye' by
Trimming just one Swiss chard leaf a day

Or refrigerating the eggplant's face
Which absorbs all the words they didn't say
When he died on the table or in his sleep.
And you, failing to put death to bed
Despite the patches of caskets tended,
Think of all this soothing in exhuming

His fingerling potatoes Thanksgiving Day
So something of him will flavor the family table.
And consider the first Christmas Eve alone
Made bearable in gently separating
His dried onion seeds from their communal blooms.
And praise, finally, the few who learn to keep

Unpicked Brussels sprouts below the snow
So, aggrieved in February, they can reach
For remaining green heads beneath the cold
And the tracks of the foraging doe so
Hollow and deep that, surely, they sow
Some of the falling, seeding moon-glow to grow . . .

For the Octogenarian Flower Arranger

Though her hands—in repose—
No longer bloom into soft sea roses,
Still her head feels like a tulip blossom
Bubbling with intoxicated honey bees
Each time she completes another bouquet's
Flowery fireworks display to skyline
The chemo patient's bedside tray;
And so she muses how her final seasons
Might be like the perennial tiger lily
Still bursting forth her soul's own orchestra
Of greens, yellows and oranges
Despite last winter's ice and snow
Seeping into the bulb of her
Bones . . . whose aches now, she prays,
Won't keep her from arranging
The bouquet of her last days
In such a way that, at ninety,
She still walks the Elysian Field
Of half-acre greenhouse in July
And, like an old, picked rose
Only needs a little aspirin,
Modest morning light,
And limestone of inspiring ode
To keep her color and bud of love
Unfurling the red petal
Of her delight-ridden tongue—
Up until that day, God bless,
She drops dead in a raised flower bed
And her last moments, as dreamed,
Are those of being swallowed
By a purple coffin of flotsam blossoms
Before sinking into the upholstery
Of compost, and tossing a bouquet
Of thanks for the way it's so easy, here,
To imagine her ashes reincarnating
Her blue eyes into morning glories

And vocal chords into loosestrife's perfume
(Singing it's aria of aroma to the bees)
That, surely, her Goldenrod-of a God
Or her Pink-Ruffled-Edged-Profusion
Of sweet Jesus climbing his trellis
Of New Testament to heaven—
Will ensure such a compassionate passing,
Within the vase of her last day,
Is perfectly arranged.

Ode to the Letter G or "Oh Mother of God Seet Jesus"

With a grin and jowls
Making cursive J
Green with envy
G's simply gorgeous
Even while grieving,
Gossiping, and grandiloquently
Prophesying gloom
And Armageddon
For every generation.
Yes, G's GQ visage
And garrulousness
So ingratiate
That we deem him
Congenial and gentrified
Even when he gratuitously
Sentences the guilty
To gallows
And guillotine;
And G's gift
To get one giddy
With the giggles
And to drown a grim
And grotesque existence
With an endless
Supply of gravy
Mutes opposition
To how he
Always leads "grace"
And grandiosely claims
That he best speaks
For all that's "good,"
"God," and "glorious"
In this great, big galaxy.
And on the anniversary
Of my grandmother's
Death, who'd have guessed,

G, I'd envy
The way you keep
Your chin up
When shipwrecked
On the island reef of "grief"
As I grapple with
A life of grace
And goodwill
Not guaranteeing
A death free
Of radiography
And the tumor's
Gratuitous growth
After she pleaded,
"Sweet Jesus,"
To just let her "go
To her grave
And God...
Yes, G, grant us
Your guts and gallantry
To give the Grim Reaper
Your same gritty grin
If we too don't go
So "gently into
That good night"
With a gloating profile
Exclaiming how
We're going to our God
Remembering all
The gifts we gave,
Ingrained, in the voices
Of the next generation.
And grandmother who died
Before I could say anything
But "gee" and "gosh"
Through eulogy

And burial, let me
Finally let go
Of the grief that's so
Gripped me as,
At the end of your ode,
My chin shapes
Into the G of saving grace
In saying: "see, now,
Your grandchild's eyes
Finally turning into
The two beautiful o's
Of "goodbye," crying . . .

Trophy Lake Trout

After that twenty-eight minute fight winding
The time dial of boat counterclockwise, his heart goes
And for months his buddies are confused
Over the karma of CPR (catch, photo and release)
Where such dharma should lengthen one's life
Or be seen as a shout out to the grandeur of their God.
They argue, now, about the metaphysics of bag limits
And, nights, find their red devil eyes trolling commentaries
About what 'you reap so shall you sow'—
Until, in their shared confusion about God's rules,
They feel in a like fight for their freshwater lives
In the inability to break free from this nagging
Twenty-pound test- line of philosophical inquiry.
Afternoons, now, one trolls with
Eckhart's "Book of Comfort" open
To erase seeing the blue sky as a lake surface which might
Suddenly open to pluck his soul from the pickerel weeds
Of his drinking buddies. Another negotiates
the horrific mystery
By considering those apostle fishermen soon thriving
After the terror and confusion over the crucifixion
Which wasn't supposed to slip their sweet Jesus into
The slick creel of eternity. But we're hooked, I think,
By their newfound tenderness in needling lures from lips
And reviving winded smallmouths before release—
Where they see themselves, now, as the fishes' Gods
Drifting in the cumulous clouds of canoes;
And where they name their hand tied flies
After the tender angels they dream might
Pull them up through their own tunnel of light
And into death's meshed net; and where, hearing
Of another unexpected angler's passing before fifty,
They think of God's own "catch n release" policy
Where the few who die and are miraculously thrown back
Often blankly stare back at all the questions we cast
Or give us back those same sad, stunned fish eyes

Also blinded by the mystery of so much sun
And holding a lifetime's bag limit of silence.

Fishing Lures

Some welcome getting skunked, so drunk
In the lodge, they can repeatedly bemoan
"How the black-spotted, uncle-josh pork frog"
Didn't entice one damn catfish to strike."

For others it's as close as they'll come
To being a poet at the podium
In crooning to passing angler in canoe
How the last rainbow attacked the

"Archer-bee, lucky-craft, splash-tail ninety
With green, stainless-steel ball bearing knees."
And, when a father advises his son
To try a "purple, floating-zoom trickle worm"

Another boy's pickerel lips open to
The allure of our wonderful words
Which we, too, have come to believe
Are small-frye versions of king salmon reality.

Oh, I'm not saying there's secret, poetry retreats
Somewhere on "Mooselookmyguntic lake"
Where men pen names of spinner baits
Then scores are held up like largemouth's' weights

At the end of the weekend derby.
But, that burly guy replacing shocks
Or downing ice-damaged trees
Likely opens that plastic tackle box

With the ceremony of a poet
Cracking open a Norton Anthology.
Yes, consider him lured to cast
The "fat bodied balsa b crank bait"

(Over the live shiners pike are striking)
Because the name will go great
With the story to his Jersey-girl fiancée
Of landing the Wiley two pounder

He's then going to bake in the new range.
And if, like him, you've also lost a dad
Who loved to fish, consider casting
His cherished "mooselook wobbler"

For the way it lures memories to hit
From those summers alone with him
Trolling the lower Richardson....
Where, sometimes, the son feels his dad

Staring through the stars' lily pads
To savor his way of playing these memories
Over the trophy largemouth bass rising
Until the day, of course, the boy finally

Finds a few beautiful words to boat
Some of those lunker feelings below
And—expressing each grievous feeling—
His words, we pray, are as soothing

As whispering "Williams Wobbler,"
"Quick-sinking Hopkins Shorty,"
Or "Stanly flat-eye, soft-skirted jig"
For the weed-ridden waters.

Bio-luminescing

Acres of single-celled algae
Illume the bay into
A phosphorescent blue
As the canoe's wake unzips
The lagoon's nightgown of moonlight;

And the female angler fish
Glows the wormy tip of her nose
So, with unhinged jaw,
She literally fishes
For her dinner.

Then there's Mrs. Jamison
Filleting "Deep Sea Life's" pages
In the anxiety of her son,
Possibly, canceling
Another nursing home

Visitation; and there's
The reading nurse's tongue
Flippering deeper
Into the dark
Paragraph's captions

As she witnessed
Her patient's eyes illume
To the amazing news
"Of the pony fish's abdomen glowing
When ascending total darkness

So he can become one
With the growing light
And invisible
To predator's eyes
Below." And after she

Dies in the night
Dark as a dragon fish
Before attack, imagine
The reading nurse
Descending two or three stories

To find another frail soul
Who too might forgive
An ungrateful child
Or somehow make this place
Feel like home

When simply hearing
How "malacosts thrive
The mile-
Deep darkness
By converting

The yellow and blue
They illume
Into infra-red rays
Their prey can't see"...

Yes, tonight, try
Seeing your life
Evolving in such a strange,
Eccentric way
After plumbing such

Lonesome depths
That you, too,
Feel completely invisible
Unless allowing
Such hope and tenderness

To effuse from your very marrow
Which, for all we know
Might also be a sign
Of the strongest
Learning to survive.

Raindrop Ode

When happiness closes its hand
And every effort to resurrect
A single bumble bee
In the abdomen
Compounds melancholy
With frustration,
I want to be you,
Raindrop,
And simply fall:
Sliver
Over
Crow feathers,
Rock n roll
Down
The back
Of oak bark,
Gopher
            Into
                    The ground—
All the way
                   Through
The earth-
              Worm's intestine
Of irrigation

To de-com-pos-ing

Stone

And bone

And wait for the sun
And a lifetime of resurrection.

III

Sweet Cells

Ode to Lettuce, or the Secret Life of Lettuce

> The single criterion of true beauty is that it increases
> On examination
>
> —*Fulke Greville, Victorian Critic*

So fragile,
We tweezer
Your seed in-
To the peat-
Pot's womb
As though
Performing
A "veggie invitro"
So—when
Your leafy fetus
Finally births
From the earth
To be wet-nursed
By the sun's
Buttermilk beams—
We're so pleased
Life's taken root
That we feel
Like a parent
Conquering
Infertility
Or a God
Seeding Eden.
Soon, too,
We post
The bony
Scarecrow
To baby-sit
When we're not
Weeding, watering,
And shoring up
The garden's

School yard
Of collapsing
Chicken wire;
Soon, too,
We're burrowing
Cups of beer
By your nursery row
So slugs choose
To pirate the booty
Of barrels of booze
Over your virgin
Leaves. And
Despite surviving
Such a tough
Adolescence
Where you never
Got to gaze
Into your biological
Mother's face
Or move into
The high-rise condo
Of a raised bed
Like the upwardly
Mobile cherry tomatoes,
You don't succumb
To the rebellious wanderlust
Of the butter-nut squash
Or become in-
Troverted, bitter,
And hard-hearted
Like the turnip.
No, lettuce, instead
You keep your head
And maintain
That Cool-Hand-
Luke demeanor

Even when weeds
Storm your
Green Bastille . . . .
So when we
Finally harvest you
To be the sea
To float the boats
Of Big Boy tomatoes
Alongside the
Eels of red onions
And stingrays
Of sliced mushrooms,
We're so amazed
With the way
You always thrive
By turning inward
In crisis
And worshiping
In the church
Of your dirt
That we believe
You in league
With any St. Assisi
Or Thoreau.
And, with dirt
Stuck in our
Sneaker soles
And our praise
Like blue cheese
Holding the
Sweet raisons
Of our admiration,
We hold your green
Glimmering globe
Up to the unseen
Constellations

And wonder
(For a moment)
Just who
Raised who.

For The Giant Pumkin Growers

This one hand pollinates the tulip-like blossoms
Then covers the fuzzy flowers with banded socks
So bees don't cross pollinate with a lesser seed.
This gourd guru bathes his in liquid calcium
Before fertilizing roots with molasses's and fish
To fuel the twenty-plus pounds they can gain in a day.

And, nights, none trusts the pumpkins' silence
So they slink through the electric fences,
Reach between the comforters of leaves, and
Brush hands over the sleepers who they believe,
Like babies, grow most in the evenings so
The only sound one might hear is the clack
Of one of the hundred-plus mouse traps
They moat around their green, medieval castles
To keep away the invading vassals of mice.

And by harvest time, each is a mid-wife
In cutting the umbilical stem before phoning the D.O.T.
To ensure there are no frost heaves or major pot holes
On the road to the weigh-in way upstate.
And the ones who don't place, run hands over fruit
As though the gourd is a teen's bruised ego
Needing consoling after being dumped
By their beau after the flower making parade . . .

But, driving home, always this odd solace grows
In the coming fairs where children run to the truck
With their faces flush as October pumpkins in sun.
There, one hollows her gourd into a dollhouse
Where girls enter through a neatly carved door
Leading to a table for tea for two; there a New Yorker
Chainsaws a giant jack-o-lantern of a face,
Mounts a tripod outside, and snaps photos
Of smiling faces sheening through the bay window of smile.

And a last guy hollows his gourd into a dory
He mounts with a two-horse outboard
To boat kids around the lake's cove;
Over eighty, how easy, he now thinks, to die
Knowing how he's so deftly carved hearts
To appreciate a life of earthworms and compost piles
So, sometimes, turning 360's, he marvels
At how fat with fascination they grow
And he desires a means to weigh the fruit
Of enthusiasm reddening their faces;

Other times—with their orange life vests
Puffing out their chests—they seem holding
So many like, inchoate seeds of promise
As they beg parents to plant next year's beans,
Cukes, corn, and zucchini. And before he retires
Let all the giant pumpkin growers, he hopes,
See this joy and fascination is what grows
The heart's own gourd-like organ
To expand so high and wide that, like the
Fascinated October child, you dream, too,
Of crawling inside and, for a while,
Making it a home while standing at full height.

Ode to Scarlet Runner Beans Rising Up the Eight Foot Trellis

As the ten-foot row of pole beans approaches
The tip of the six-foot, stringed trellis,
I glean a great, green sail being raised
By a crew of nectar-drunk bees scrambling over
The slick, rocking deck of squash leaves below.

And when the lithe dragonflies gymnastic
Over the scaffolding of stems while
Hummingbirds alight the blossoms' crows-nests,
I imagine I'm captain of this ship
Where sweet beets, radishes, and turnips

Are valuable as any spice, dark rum,
And molasses stowed away in a hold.
Note, too, how I risk life and limb scrambling over
The deck through rain and hurricane gales
In order to shore up the masts of the trellis.

Note, too, how I'll pace the rows each dusk
To keep whitetails from pirating lettuce
Then speeding away their bodies' dories
With their legs' four, long, limber oars.
But, like most voyages to the Spice Islands

My growing season, I admit, is pretty routine
As my crew of insects and worms performs
Without the slightest sign of mutiny
Despite how I walk all over them
Through the droughts, floods, and cold.

Any wonder, come August, I leave
My second-mate scarecrow at the wheel
While I pen the garden log's daily entries.
Any wonder, by Labor Day, I'm nipping
A dram of rum and reading by the radio—

Though, before sleep, walking the deck briefly
  And, even when I see whole rows of beets
And squash hollowed by mice and moles,
      Still feel the journey is still worth it
For the way— in clear fall air— I can gaze

   At spirit spouts of trees spraying their green,
And meteors porpoising the Milky Way's Sea
   While the ballooning harvest moon is so beautiful
That the heart, too, realizes ripeness
     And into its dim lit harbor does berth . . .

Observations on the Garden, Fourth of July

As pole beans bottle rocket bursting buds
Into the horizon of chicken wire, suddenly
I marvel at the fireworks of my beloved veggies
Celebrating this great, green diverse nation
Where Southern collards abide neighboring
Yankee broccoli—while Waspy, sweet corn aids
Humble pole beans seeking like Wall Street
Heights. And when the Italian squash explode
Their blooms' M-80's, I see my immigrants' zeal
In moving from greenhouse indentured servitude
To thriving in their high-rise, raised bed homes—
So that, now, I'm the Founding Father of this garden
Who brilliantly scribed the constitution of compost pile
And polices the fenced-in borders for raiding
Woodchucks and tunneling skunks. Oh MLK
Would set off a fireworks of words if taking in
My companion planting's seamless integration
Of black bean beside white carrot! And Hamilton,
I think, would admire our green-leafed currency
Always backed by the gold standard of organic
Seeds! Tomorrow, then, I'll wake early to resume
This Westward expansion over the Great Plains
Of half-acre field where not one native burdock
Or hollyhock is exterminated. And, nights, I'll scribe
A State of the Union calling for all patriotic produce
"To imagine a nation where each humble pea
Has access to a trellis and our much praised
Upward mobility." And planting myself deep
Into the dirt of service to my people,
May I create a legislative body of loam
Perfectly balancing the two major parties
Of acid and alkaline so that all feel
Their congress of roots can thrive;
And may the history book of garden log praise
How we overcame the Pearl Harbor
Of Japanese beetles raiding our island nation

Soon after we fought the Huns of woodchucks
On foreign soil before their tanks in-
Fitrated our burgeoning cities of kale.
Now, though, time for some of Jefferson's wine
And to just let my people put up their rooves
Of blooms and split shingles of leaves—
While the pioneering pumpkins and cucumbers
Fulfill our manifest destiny in wheeling
The covered wagon trains of their leaves
Through the Rockies of wild blackberries
And, tomorrow, I finally recognize the beacon
We're becoming to all oppressed seedlings
By placing a great torch in the scarecrow's hand
To call forth every immigrant kernel adrift
In the ocean of breeze (or stowed in the vole's
Furry hold) to choose this greatest of lands
From seed to shinning seed.

Upon Hearing that "Bread is the Way Sun Enters Our Body"

I feel this need to knead on my knees
And praise the daily "tran-sun-stantiation"
Of sun into whole grain calories via
The Holy ghost of yeast. And kudos

To pepperoni pizza dough now morphing
Into these acned teens of Helios
While the bread sticks become nothing-less
Than batons of this God-force handed off

To hungry loved ones so, in mere contemplation
Of a "single grain of whole wheat,"
They might finally cross the
Finishing line into the divine!

Oh yes, bless the shamans of our bakers
Keeping those stone oven temples' fired
To coax golden Goddesses inside honey wheat
To continue illumining the skyline of every slice!

And after we caffeinate conversations
By singing how each sweet portly, pastry
"Is just sun made up in so much make-up"—
Or by declaring "the solar flare of each éclair"—

Or by shimmying in kind to "the northern lights'
Cosmic cursive espied in the marbled rye"—
Consider, finally, the sourdough's soul's
Own second rising when musing

How that same sun beams through
The doughy body's own celestial abode
So our neurons feel the same heat
As those distant rings of Neptune do—

And our membranes glow for the same reason
As any of the solar system's marvelous moons—
And sun, bread, and body s are now just one
String-laden cosmos-in-expansion—

Heeding us, surely, to feel the vitamin d of delight
As her hand, say, alights and tans your thigh—
Or to know the solar radiation of a soul
So freely giving love over to your blue being—

Which fathoms, now, how that sacred moment
Of silence before breaking open the loaf
Is heightened by looking into one another's eyes
And recognizing all the sunshine in disguise.

The Dry Stone Waller Revisits Spring's Surfacing Fieldstones

Before stones of eggs hatch feathered heads
Or tadpoles eel from gel-a-ti-nous embryos,
Fieldstones crown the brown, thawing ground

And, after decades of mid-wifing stones,
I'm so smitten with my youthful marvel exhumed
In desiring, like a child around puppies,

To lift each newborn up, turn them over,
And run hands over wet heads and torsos,
That, over supper, my wife spies the young buck

Who, long ago, abruptly frost heaved her life
And, that evening, she loves me so much
That, as I thrust up and up and up in lust,

I'm like a rising stone given a second life,
And I welcome hands gripping my schist hips
Before feet scamper the granite shoulders

And, when it's over, one warm fingertip
Alights the forehead's cliff, slides down the
Face-wall of the jowls, and, like the lost hiker

In the White Mountains, seems to know home
Is somewhere close, now that she stares into
That familiar old-man-on-the-mountain nose.

The Dragonfly Biologist Falling in Love

Because she thinks love, too,
Is threatened with slow extinction
Despite it's like translucent wings,
Her slow rising to romance's promise is
A dragonfly nymph crawling up reed stock
After five years of moon walking the bottom of a pond;

And she imagines his first tender strokes
As those first warm rays dissolving
The emerging nymph's armored encasing
So the winged, inchoate fetus inside
Can birth from behind the cervix
Of those enormous Darth Vader eyes;

And when she's tortured by thoughts
Of everything that could go wrong
She's schooled to think of predatory birds
Circling after one swallow-swoon
Alerts them to the cad fly appetizers hatching
Over the fractured plates of lily pads;

But when she tempers his expectations
By explaining the years of underwater life
Prior to the dragonfly's brief five weeks of flight,
His carpe diem nature overtakes
And she finds herself, on dates, netted
By his surprised embraces from behind.

Later, she acclimates to the strangers
Watching their playful foreplay
As though in frolicking they, too, shine
An aqua green or lupine blue.
And the day after they rise together
From his bed, may he follow her

To the remote bogs and ponds
To press the netted wings together
Before lifting the creature for measuring;
And may he marvel, like her, at the two
Pair of wings working in perfect unison
While the ten thousand lensed eyes

Are alert to everything for 360 degrees;
And when one—upon release—
Alights his shoulder, may he still,
Like a child playing One, Two, Three Red Light,
Move his eyes enough to see the way
She rests, transfixed, by his side, smiling

And unwilling, too, to move, or breathe, or speak
Whether it's curiosity, exhaustion, or love
Keeping the mysterious dragonfly in their life.

Ode to the Letter O or "U.F.O.: Unidentified Flying Ode"

Out of all the vowels
O is most noted
For beating out the
Ambitious A
And egomaniacal I
To win the lead role
In the production of "poem,"
"Othello," "God," and "Soul."
We feel so close to O
For how he never loses his soothing tone
Even while echoing
Through T,K, and G's dissonant boroughs—
We shape O
Into a perfect circle
And make him the soul
Of "cosmos" and "holy"
For how intoning "OOOhhhm"
Opens us to consciousness,
God, and the ineffable
Where the soul feels peaceful,
Whole, at hOme . . . But
So well-known
For Opening "third eyes"
And being the only vowel
Who can bring "word,"
"Good" and "God" into the world
Causes O to suffer over-exposure:
"Oh" what echoes when exposed
To your first lover's genitals
And, later, in the ecstasy
Of your first orgasm;
"Oh" intoned upon seeing
The mortician close
The casket over
The tongue of your
Grandmother's torso;

And the "oh" your mother echoed
When conceiving you
Was the same "oh" she screamed
When they cut you
From the o of her
Bleeding womb . . . You see O
Circles you everywhere go
Until it's impossible to escape
The orbit and gravitational pull
Of planet O—O the verbal toll
Paid before motoring
Words of rage and marvel
At six-thousand syllables per hour!—
O the traffic circle
All models of emotions spin
Until merging into the
Bumper-to-bumper syntax
Of a sentence! And, initially, O
It confused me to exhale
Your same beautiful tone
On the evening she told me she loved me
And on the evening she told me
She loved another soul.
I perceived the mysterious
Crop circle of you as opportunistic
In overturing so many disparate emotions!
I wanted you only to speak
For joy, hope, or sorrow
So I could trust the role
You played in all the words
You wheeled into the world!
But now O, as age slowly reveals
How each new love
Holds some old sorrow
And each old sorrow stows
Some new love in its hold,

You seem to resemble
The mystical Tao
The monk divines behind
The masks of good and evil/
Joy and sorrow/ male and female!
You seem whole, all-knOwing—
The only self-actualized vowel
Reconciled with its shadOw!
And so O, at the end of your ode
I finally come full circle
And give up this quest to decode you
Like the human genome
And, vowing simply, now, that the O
Of my poems also work to enfold both
The howling love dogs without a bone
And couples whose bliss glooms their souls
Maybe begin loving
As unconditionally as you
And give the world back
A little of what she's owed.

The Baby Blue Whale's Blues Solo

Growing around two-hundred pounds a day—
Over eight pounds per hour—so every two tides
It puts on the weight of a heavyweight boxer
Or a finalist for the title of Mr. Universe,
Consider the potential to see that calf grow
If we dove while he suckled the four-hundred liters
Of milk comprising his daily bottle. Yes, putting on
Three ounces a minute for the first month of a life
Where he'll mature to twice the size of the
Largest dinosaur, consider how we could
Place hands over the calf's boat of back
And come oh so close to feeling its flesh
Flower like a slowly, inflating life raft—almost
Watch the blow hole and eyes blossom as though
In amazement of its own enormous growth—
Almost see the whale's tail reaching out to us . . .
And, if we dove knowing the mother's heart
Is large as an auto and pumps eight tons of blood
Through arteries a human can swim through,
Consider our marvel growing at a like vast pace
In imagining her heartbeat and song then
Sonagramming our chest. And, as layered thick,
Now, with marvel, as this mother and calf are
With flesh, consider our hesitancy to surface
As, in that moment of deep sea reverie, we
Finally feel the soul's expansive potential
And lament how, despite such promise,
It, too, frequently remains submerged
In a body that's mostly salt and sea
And whose evolutionary tale stretches all the way
Back to an age when we swam daily with whales.

The Song of Our Cells —after Reading *The Intimate Universe*

Shedding around five million cells a day—
Over two-hundred thousand per hour—

Bleeding a trail of molecules
While speeding in the convertible,

Amazing how the body maintains
A legal, "photo ID" while re-

Growing a new stomach lining
Every five days or so

And, by the end of a trimester,
A whole new set of bones.

Yes, avalanching thousands of cells
From the cliffs of the knuckles

Just in scratching an itch,
Amazing how the body persists

And doesn't picket for a five-day work week
After laboring forty days and nights

To renovate our two-hundredth liver;
And seldom calls in sick

After gift wrapping us in new skin
By the deadline of each new moon;

And, under pressure to replace
Each brain cell before the year is through,

Doesn't erase the memory of our first kiss
Or the D.N.A. on how to fashion our cowlick—

Until, by the end of the body's yearly cycle,
It's renewed 98% of our 75 trillion cells

So, on our eightieth birthday,
We can celebrate how we've outlived our self

For the eightieth time in a row
While gloating how our eight-thousandth stomach swells

With the cake we're tasting
With our six-thousandth set of sweet cells

As we frost the frosting of our name
With thousands of unseen pieces of the body

In the continuing battle to blow out
The one trick candle.

Some Words on Birds and Borders

Let's praise all the world's birds
Unconcerned with shots and passports
As they cross disputed borders
Then refuse to seek permission to
Land on the river's moonlit landing strip.

And let's sing of those crazy, Canada geese
Violating North American Trade agreements
As their bellies import unknown grains
And they don't stop for the bomb sniffing dogs.
And see how no winged being heeds

A "no fly zone" between warring counties
Where one private notes "soldiers
Turning into birders as they lord over
The no man's land" where grouse seek spouses
Along the mine-laced gravel roads

And falcons let their young fly over
The steel trees of anti-aircraft artillery.
And imagine, now, the seeds of peace sown
By the peacock caught between cross-fire
Or by the mother cardinal spied nesting over

The killing fields; and you—birder of words—
Unsure if you can fly into this altruism's altitude
Where flocks of hopeful thoughts are flushed
From the single thrush admired through
The sniper's scope, when did the B-52 of blue heron

Ever fail to drop, into river or pond,
Anything but it's body's beautiful bomb?

Two Birds Trapped in the Screened in Porch

Forgetting their torn-screen   portal-like entry
They panic from lantern to   hanging ski limb
And fear a giant, marauding   hawk wing
Unfolding when I slowly open   the door.

Unwilling to scare them to their   soft suicides
After watching eight ounce bodies,   in retreat,
Ricochet off the coop-like screen   whose wire
Plunks them of vital plumage,   I feel like

A parrot trapped inside my   cottage cage
As my own frustrating trills   now echo . . .
For a while, too, my eyes beak   about the room
For a broom long enough to reach   between the two doors

And trip the handle for both   our getaways.
For a while, too, my mind is   a rare bird of paradise
Thinking of calling my neighbor   for coffee
Where, after she opens the door,   I'll feign

A like amazement over the   two birds
That did fireworks from the   front porch.
Finally, though, I "Great Escape" out   my own
Bedroom window, ferret   to their coop,

And— after opening their   escape way
So they can restock their   chickadee flock—
Find that I've kept the damn   cottage locked.
Now, with bedroom window too high   to reach,

My arms wing over the locked   kitchen window
And my bird-beady eyes stare through   the pane
To lament my lost   native landscape
Where lush bananas hang and books safely   nest

Above the desk. Strange, though—   after snaking
Through the cracked, unlocked bathroom   window
And arriving inside with a   back crick
Returned to cricket its   fused discs—

How I flap my arms in celebration   and skip
From room to room like they from   limb to limb
Until that cardinal of a heart inside   the rib cage
Sings me awake for the second time today.

The Glass Blower of Birds

Blowing out breasts with nothing but breath
He's a god working the hot firmaments
And soon draws in flocks of ornithologists

Who marvel at tweezers teasing out perfect beaks
And the swifts crafted in less than a minute.
But more than watching birds fly from the forge—

Or seeing the "rabbit-from-hat" magic
Of egrets hatching from eggs of molten glass—
Is the endangered species taking wing

And filling the bird watchers with spirit breath
As a creature (who escaped their glass)
Unfolds her wings from the leafy limbs of flames.

Now their blood gets hot wanting to touch
A being who, too, comes from biblical dust;
Now they feel the miracle of unseen wings

Unfolding from their own molten torsos
In a desire to live months in an old tree
To save a certain Bird of Paradise....

Nights, one sleeps more peacefully feeling
These imitations are just what's needed
To increase our reverence enough to clean

The air and preserve those dying forests;
Another perches his rare bird over her bureau
So, drifting to sleep, she hears the chirps

Of the one long extinct in the remote valley.
And a third places his rare bird in a cage
Where it's safe from cat paws and earthquakes

And, when he wakes, it's always so life-like
That he's certain it gloams with all the souls
Of those poor birds passing after spying

A great green tree or potential mate re-
Flected back from the spotless window's glass
Which, though not cracking, shatters, sadly,
A little master-piece.

Encounter with Roofer

When he drops his hammer for a noon sandwich
He's like a Buddha atop a grand stupa
As bare feet set over the eaves while he reads
Thich Nhat Hahn's "Peace is Every Step."

And Thinking his earlier noise bad karma
For making my morning writing an uphill rhyme
I sherpa into the sacred space of his lunch break
And discover he's read the whole of Kornfield

And, like me, practices that walking meditation
Where he imagines the soles of his feet
Massaging the vertebrae of mother earth's
Tectonic plates. Now, sharing cool aid

And khoans, we're like Tu Fu and Li Po high
Atop some remote mountain peak shading
A river below eroding time and stone.
Later that afternoon, in the silence

Which announces the end of his work day,
I'll climb a second time with the gift of a Hahn line
Decreeing "rainwater is the master bodhisattva."
He'll reply "those who say they know, don't know;

Those who say they don't know, know."
And though we won't exchange emails
To meet for a tea ceremony
Or to play our Tibetan bowls

As I help him throw the remaining shingles
Into the backed up truck below
Then gladly tie down the sliding ladder,
I know the leak of a future sadness has been sealed

Ode to Happy

Speaking happy, consider the
Snuggling p's as puppies
Ecstatic to be released

From the word's cramped pound
Closed in, say, by the gate of h
Guarded by the law abiding a.

Yes your elocution frees
Two dogs to sniff through
The sentences' streets

Then chew on the
Phonemes' bones
Until molars break through

The soft-marrowed ecstasy
In "happy to be alive;
Happy to know you."

Oh the O.E.D. claims:
"Feeling or showing pleasure;
A sense of confidence in

Or satisfaction with a person,
Arrangement or situation."
But no, "I'm happy" released

From the choke-collared throat,
Licks each face clean
Then leaps onto strangers' laps

Without invitation or shame
Over her wet, musky coat.
. Yes, love her like the dog

You only got after begging
Like a starved dog
And promising to walk,

Brush, and feed her twice daily!
Or love her like the mongrel
Who only growls and howls

When you fail to offer an embrace
Through the pound's steel cage.
And when happiness fails

To heed your commands
To heal, sit and stay—
(Despite how you toss her

The milk bone of an ode)—
Think of your beloved collie
Only bolting because she

Can't resist the Elysian field
Of loosestrife and milkweeds
Alit with butterflies:

What grace in her circling
By way of coaxing you
To join in the chase

Where she believes—
If you follow in tow—
You'll, too, soon scent

The deer bedding down
In the cool pine needles
In a happiness only they can know.

The Dry Stone Waller on the Major League Baseball Player Who, During His First Season, Left the Big Leagues to Return to Walling

** inspired by John Clough of Brooklyn, Maine*

No one asking 'why stones over the Astros
Or if gloving grounders returned his love
Of fielding rocks frost heaved from cornfields'

For, as he waxed poetic about the talent
In laying the first straight row of stones
Equaling that of making a bunt hug

A third base line, each of us realized
We'd not led such dire, Minor League lives
In some dumb, Toledo-Mud-Hen of a city

Until Bruce—by the All-Star break—spoke
Of a perfectly layed capstone echoing
Like the crack of a home-run bat

And Phil— by the dog days of August—
Mused about our wall's pitch more exact,
Than an All-Star's change-up over the plate—

So, by the World Series, we were so pleased
By our like double-play ballet in setting
The hips, shoulders, and torso just so

To turn and toss those twenty pound rocks,
That, laying our season's last stones,
We playfully tipped our John Deer caps

To the screaming orioles and blue jays
And felt such gratitude over the fact
That Tom, in spring, would call us back

That the last stone our fingers slipped over
Turned each of us into that clutch Mr. October
Sliding face-first safe over a felt for home plate.

The Dry Stone Waller Walling in the Old Town Cemetery

In rising walls I spy a giant coffin
For a late, open casket wake where god
Weeps over "wife Jane taken from child,"
Though, in old maples' roots nourished by de-
Composed caskets' remains, I too spy
"Newlyweds dying in honeymoon fire"
Re-incarnating into leaves with such view
Of Lake Winnipesauke that they, too,
Possibly divine God's design in
These brief lives of living on nothing but light
And so I celebrate the fallen leaves, in spring,
Returning as iris who—peering over
The wall— turn this coffin into a cradle
Ever so gently rocking my joy awake.

For the Organ Donor's Widow Meeting the Man Who Received Her Deceased Husband's Corneas

—Since 2003 Nicole Folden has visited Texas, Minnesota, and Wisconsin meeting the people whom her husband's organ saved

—On average, 40 to 60 people are saved or have their lives greatly improved from each body donation.

Though pained to see her ex's eyes
As they meet for lunch in South Philly,
They exchange emails and, weeks later,
A photo of him and his wife arrives

Which the widow sets beside the frame
Of the Mainer—who received the lungs—
Crossing the 5-k finishing line in Bangor.
Six months further, she prints the grinning mug

Sent by the heart recipient's oldest son
Who thanks her "for the granddad his kids will have."
The Christmas after that fruit cakes still come
From the pancreas recipient in Houston—

Until some warn that denial might inspire
All those long-distance minutes to the Milwaukee teen
Who received the marrow and beat the leukemia.
But at the baptism for the son

Of the Teamster who received his kidney
The widow feels herself fit so perfectly
Inside all the hugs freely given
That she imagines herself as a liver or lung

Immersed into the warmth of new body
And quickly achieving synchrony
With trinity of heart, kidneys and arteries
As the children, to boot, call her auntie.

Now, without hesitation, she flies to meet
The Iowan who received the small intestine
Then drives all the way to the Motor City
For the liver recipient's fifth year of sobriety.

And as for me, I love how it's becoming routine
To place this story inside so many minds
Where, like a pink, perky organ, it re-orchestrates
Our blocked and chaotic body of thoughts to flow

In such a way that a healthy, hopeful mind is restored.
And I love how sharing this amazing tale
Doesn't require a PhD and sleepless residency
Before transplanting its healing properties

Into the brains of complete strangers
Then sealing it inside with the sutures of these lines.....
And I love, finally, how her engagement
To the kidney recipient's cousin

Causes pulses to strengthen and faces to flush
Until, even the most cynical of us
Is inspired to donate her story
To the old curmudgeon of a neighbor

Or the misanthrope of co-worker
Who, too, walk away with more pep in their step
And nights, sometimes, stare up at the sky
To imagine all the harvested organs flying

From Syracuse to Duluth—Boise to Austin—
And saving so many lives despite
All that time—between bodies—packed
Like a cheap six-pack, on ice.

Acknowledgments

Grateful acknowledgement is made to the following presses in which some of these poems previously appeared in chapbook format:
Finishing Line Press, "Stone By Stone: Poems about the Art of Dry Stone Walling," Leah Maines, Publisher
Moon Pie Press, "Unidentified Flying Does," Alice Persons, Publisher
Sheltering Pines Press, "Bio-luminescing," Annie Farnsworth, Publisher

Grateful acknowledgement is made to the following journals and online zines in which some of these poems previously appeared:

Spoon River Poetry Review: Ode to Teenage Hairdos in June, The Dry Stone Waller Muses about Cosmology
Poetry East Magazine: The Dry Stone Waller Walling in the Town Cemetery
The Hamilton Stone Review: The Dry Stone Waller Gathering Spring's Surfacing Fieldstones, The Dry Stone Waller on the Major League Baseball Player Who, During His First Season, Left the Big Leagues to Return to Walling
Words and Images: Watching the Man with No Hands Teach the Boy with No Hands how to Fish
Identity Theory and A Sense of Place: Collected Maine Poems: Highly Autistic Bagboy Asking Our Check-out Girl
Ascent Aspirations: Encounter with Roofer, Some Words on Birds and Borders
Cardinal Flower: Ode to Lettuce, Ode to Scarlet Runner Beans, Some Words on Birds and Borders, Two Birds Trapped in a Screened in Porch, For Earthworms
A Year of Being Here: Poems on Mindfulness: Encounter with Roofer
Off the Coast: For the Russian Rainbow Trout Farmer
MWPA Honorable Mention, Kate Barnes: Stephen Hawking Talking

Anthologies:
Port City Poems Anthology: Ode to Teenage Hairdos in June
Full Moon Rising: The Best of Moon Pie Press: Ode to Teenagers Hairdos in June, Ode to O, Ode to the Letter G, Teaching Simile at a Midwest University

Explorers: A Collection of Contemporary Literature: Teaching Simile at a Midwest University
Poets Guide to New Hampshire, 2008: The Dry Stone Waller Walling in the Town Cemetery
Agreeable Friends: Contemporary Animal Poetry, Moon Pie Press: Watching the First-time Seeing Eye Dog Trainer Part with Her First Dog
The Wildest Peal: Contemporary Animal Poetry, Moon Pie Press: The Baby Blue Whale's Blues Solo

CD's
A Big Bang of Bards: Poems from Portland-area Poets: The Baby Blue Whale's Blues Solo
Port Poems: Poems by Kennebunk and Kennebunkport Poets: Ode to the Letter G
Beat Nights at the Electric Cave: Poems Celebrating the Beat-night Reading Series: Song of My Cells

Thanks, too, to Nancy Henry who generously read through this manuscript and pruned, sectioned, and ordered the poems in a way which, I hope, makes it cohesive and nurturing.

Finally, much thanks to everyone involved in the vibrant poetry communities of Portland and Portsmouth where so many friendships were forged and where so many of these poems—through love, support and listening—came to fruition.

Dennis Camire is an instructor at Central Maine Community College and is on the board of Maine Poetry Central which curates the Portland Poet Laureate Program and The Sun Journal's series, In Verse: Maine Places and People. He lives in West Paris Maine.